Investing For Beginners

Ten Tips For Successful Investing

By Ezra Carter

I0404984

Copyright @2017

All rights reserved. No part of this book may be reproduced in any form or by any means without permission in writing from the publisher, .

If you like my book, please leave a positive review on Amazon. I would appreciate it a lot. Thanks!

BONUS IN THE BACK:

Take a look at my other book too. This is the title:

Real Estate Investing: 50 Tips To Get You Started In Successful Real Estate Investing

Contents:

Introduction

Chapter 1: Types of Investments

Chapter 2: Why Invest?

Chapter 3: How To Make Sense of Investing

Chapter 4: Beginning To Invest

Chapter 5: Stocks and Shares

Chapter 6: Futures

Chapter 7: Options Trading

Chapter 8: Financial Education

Chapter 9: Managing Your Money

Chapter 10: Ten Easy Steps to Investing

Chapter 11: Understanding Indexing

Conclusion

Introduction

Do dreams of being able to retire early (or at least a reasonable age) appeal to you? Have you thought about investing but are unsure where to start? Finally, have you ever wondered how wealthy people gained their wealth and were able to continuously grow it? If so, this is the book for you. We are going to cover the basics of investing and hopefully answer questions as well as ease any fears you may have. Finances in general tend to be stressful for most people. Investing and the stock market are intimidating to many. Once you have read this book and understand some of the basic concepts and terminology, you are going to feel much more comfortable and will be ready for your first investment.

Of course, it is important to mention that investing is no a scheme to get rich quickly. Ensuring that your personal finances are under control will take work, and there is going to be a learning curve. The outcome of financial success is going to outweigh the difficult times you might experience on your road to investing. Many people believe that banks or investment professionals move your money around without your knowledge or understanding. That is simply not true. This book will cover the use of stock brokers and brokerage firms, but we are also going to provide you with simple steps to investing on your own.

No matter your lifestyle, personality type or interests, this book is going to help you understand investing and how you grow your money by letting it work for you. This book is going to introduce you to the types of investments that are great for beginners, introduction to the stock market as well as strategies to help you discover what types of investments are best for you. We hope you enjoy all the wonderful tips this book has to offer!

Chapter 1: Types of Investments

There are numerous ways to invest, and this chapter is going to briefly define the most popular trends in investing.

First, there are bank products. Credit Unions and banks provide their customers with safe and easy ways to build their savings accounts. Any transactions completed through a bank or credit union are federally insured, which means it is easy for the consumer to get to their money without any trouble. The only downfall of using banks or credit unions to invest is that the interest earned tends to be low, meaning it will take longer to build up savings or get much in return as far as your investments go.

Most banking institutions offer Savings Accounts, Certificates of Deposit (commonly referred to as CDs), or Money Market Accounts.

1. Savings Accounts – These types of accounts are insured through the FDIC and pay interest, allowing the investor to make as many deposits as they'd like whenever they choose. If you set up an account that has withdrawal restrictions, you are more likely to earn higher interest and be less likely to withdraw money to spend frivolously.
2. Money Market – These are accounts that are similar to savings or deposit accounts. These have slightly higher interest, and while checks may be written from a money market account, they are limited.

3. Certificates of Deposit – CDs give the investor predictability in the way of knowing what kind of return they are going to get on their investment. The interest rates are higher than that of a traditional savings or money market account. Money cannot be taken from a CD without steep penalties, making it easy to avoid spending. The penalties tend to be for a predetermined period of time and the majority of CDs are insured.

Another common form of investing is the use of bonds. These are loans investors make to businesses, government or other organizations and in return, the investor gets interest payments, generally paid over a specified period of time. There are all kinds of bonds like agency bonds, municipal bonds, treasuries, and corporate bonds. Additionally, there are also several kinds of bond mutual funds.

When investing in bonds or bond mutual funds, there is the risk of losing money, particularly when purchasing an individual bond and you find yourself needing to sell it before it matures. The price of mutual funds can fluctuate, same as stock mutual funds. The type of risk will vary depending on what kind of bond you purchase.

There are many types of bonds including US Treasury Securities, TIPS and STRIPS, and US Savings Bonds. Bonds can be purchased for as little as 25 dollars, but they do not mature quickly and earn interest based on the United States economy. When it comes to bonds, it is best to do quite a bit of research and choose which will be best for your investment.

Stocks is one of the more common forms of investment. The prices of any stock can fluctuate over the course of a day, a week, a month, or a year as the demand for the stock purchased rises and falls. Obviously, there are risks when choosing to invest in stocks including the failure of a company in which you have invested. When choosing to invest in stocks, first timers should consult a broker, one with a great reputation for earning his or her clients respect and making them money. There are hundreds of books on trading stocks if you are so inclined to check into that yourself. Know that buying and selling stock is not as easy as it sounds and make sure your stocks are only purchased after thoroughly researching the company in which you choose to invest.

Investment funds are another form of investing. They pool money from several investors and invest by using a certain strategy. The funds for this type of investment come in several different types, all with different features. Mutual funds, closed-end funds, or unit investment trusts must be registered with the SEC (Securities and Exchange Commission) as an investment company. Below are a couple of funds investment funds and a brief description of what they are.

1. Mutual Funds – This is what is known as an *open-end* investment company who continuously allows its shares to be purchased by the public. Those who

invest can *redeem* their shares either from the mutual fund or through a broker of the fund.

2. ETFs (Exchange Traded Funds) – These are a combination of conventional stocks and mutual funds. It is similar to a mutual fund in that the ETF is a pooled investment offering investor's interest in a portfolio that is professionally managed and diversified. ETF shares are not like mutual funds in that they are traded like on the stock exchange like traditional stocks and can be sold or purchased during the trading day at prices as the fluctuate.

Another form of investing, which is not quite as well known to most people is that of insurance annuities. This is a contract between the insurance company and the investor in which the company will make periodic payments to you which can begin immediately or at some predetermined point in the future. Annuities can be purchased either through premiums, which are a series of payments or with one lump-sum payment. These types of investing are generally used as a way to help save for retirement.

The two most common forms of annuities are fixed and variable, both of which will be detailed a little more below. There is a third type of annuity known as an indexed annuity (also referred to as equity indexed annuity).

1. Fixed Annuities – This is an insurance product with a guaranteed rate of return based on life expectancy, age at the time

the policy is purchased, interest rates, and some other factors. The good thing about fixed annuities is that the company can guarantee the rate of return through the interest rate and what the investor will be paid out. Although the word fixed means something that stays in place that does not necessarily apply to the fixed annuity. This can change over time, and your contract will detail whether or not that will happen.

2. Variable Annuities – These are investments that contain insurance features. They let the investor choose from mutual funds, and the value of the annuity depends on how the funds you chose to invest in perform. Like the fixed

annuity, the variable can be purchased with either one payment or a series of payments known as premiums. The variable annuity's rate of return will change with the money market funds, stocks, and bonds that were chosen when the policy was purchased. Within the variable annuity, you will find three standard features that cannot be found within the fixed annuity. They are tax-deferred treatment of all earnings throughout the year, death benefits, and a payout option providing income for life that is guaranteed.

3. Indexed Annuities – While less common, this type of annuity has features of both the fixed and variable annuities. These

are complex and have a guaranteed minimum interest rate in addition to an interest rate that is synced up with the market index. They are based on indexes that are widely known like the S&P 500 Stock Price Index. They can use other indexes as well that are representative of other parts of the market. The interest rate being guaranteed with indexed annuities comes with more risk, but at the same time, the potential for higher returns. There is less risk than the variable annuity, however.

Finally, we will close this chapter with a few other options for investing.

1. Retirement funds such as 401k or Roth IRAs.

2. Options trading.
3. Commodity Futures.
4. Security Futures.
5. Alternative and Complex Products.
6. Insurance.

Ultimately, finding the option or options that work best for you might require some trial and error. However, once you have found the investment options that work, stick with it. Whether it is for savings, retirement or anything else, the money paid out from your investments will be well worth the effort.

Chapter 2: Why Invest?

Based on the types of investments, we discussed in the previous chapter, you might be wondering why investing is worth your while. There are so many reasons, but one you should consider is not having to work for the rest of your life. When it comes down to it, there are really only two ways to make money. You can either work, or you can have assets and investments work for you. If you keep your money stashed under your mattress as opposed to investing it, the money is not working for you, and it will be impossible to have anything more than what you save. When you invest, you get that money to make more money when it earns interest.

Whether you decide to invest in stocks, mutual funds, options, or any of the others, we covered in Chapter 1, the objective remains the same and that is to invest in things that are going to make money for you later in life. If your goal is to retire in Fiji or send your kids to a great college, investing money early in is going to help you get to those financial goals.

Investing helps you to grow your money. Stocks, bonds, and other types of investments will provide you with returns that are going to earn more money in the long term. Investing lets you grow your wealth over time.

It can also help you save for retirement. It would be a waste of time and effort if you spent 40 years working and were unable to save any money for the day you retired. No one should or can work until they die. Investing your retirement fund in stocks, real estate, and businesses mutual funds is going to give you money that will allow you to retire and not have to worry about how you will be able to continue to live. Depending on how old you are when you decide to invest, you can decide what type of risk to take. At a younger age, you can play the market and invest in things that are higher risk. In general, the greater the risk, the greater the return. As you grow older, however, it is wiser to be conservative with your investments.

Investing can also help you to earn higher returns. If you are simply saving in a typical savings account with a bank, the interest earned on that account is not going to grow your money well enough over time. With a higher rate of return, you will earn more money. Investing will allow for higher rates of return than any savings account.

Another great reason to invest is to help you achieve your financial goals. With higher rates of return than a traditional savings account, you will be able to use that money for purchasing a home or car, putting your kids through college, or even starting your own business.

You may not be aware that investing vehicles such as 401k can be built upon pretax money. By actively investing in your 401k, you can qualify for pretax earnings meaning more of your money is going to work for you. The great thing about 401k is that most companies will match your investment adding to your savings.

As we previously touched on, investing can help you start or expand your business. Investing early on is an integral part of starting a business. There are investors who choose to support business owners and help create new products or jobs.

Now that we have provided you with some reasons to invest, let us talk about some of the most common pitfalls to avoid.

1. Starting late. We touched on this a little earlier. The later in life you invest, the less risk you are able to take. The earlier you start, the better off you are.
2. Doing nothing. Although there is nothing guaranteeing you will earn millions of dollars on your returns, one thing is certain. Doing nothing will earn you

nothing. Investing does take time and patience, but in the long run, you will have money to use as you please.

3. Do not invest before you pay of credit card debt. If you have saved up some money and have credit card debt, pay it off before you invest. Most credit cards have high interest rates, starting around 15%. If you have $10,000 to invest, but you also have $10,000 in credit card debt with that 15% interest, minimum monthly payments are going to literally get you nowhere. Pay the debt off, rebuild your savings, and then invest.

4. Investing short term. This is okay if you are going to need that money in the short term. It is wiser to invest money in stocks

you are not going to need to touch for a minimum of 3 years. It is better if the money is not accessible for 5 years or more. If you plan on investing to save for a down payment for a house or take a lavish vacation, money market funds or CDs are the best for short-term investments.

5. Turning down free money. No one would turn down 10 bucks if someone offered it to them. However, if you have not yet signed up for your company's 401k benefit, that is exactly what you are doing. Companies who offer this investment benefit match up to a certain percentage, which is free money. Always take

advantage of any employer match programs that are offered.

6. Play it safe. We touched on this previously when we discussed age. If you are younger, invest in stocks. There is plenty of time for you to go through the roller coaster ride of ups and downs in the stock market, and in the long run, it will pay off. As you get older, move those stocks into bonds. Those are safer and have less risk, which is important for those who are using their investments as income once they have retired.

7. Going wild. Just like playing it safe, taking unnecessary risks is the other extreme. Even if you are younger and are ready to take some of those risks we discussed

previously, do so cautiously. Never put all your money into one stock that might fail.

8. Collectibles or lotto. These are not investments. If collecting old cars or comic books is a hobby of yours, that would be perfect. However, if selling all of your collectibles when you reach retirement age worked for everyone, there would be no need for the stock market or any other retirement investment funds. Collectibles are a hobby, so do not count on those to make money when you are ready to retire. The same applies to lotto tickets. Gambling from time to time is a choice, but it is not a way to hope for the jackpot and not have to worry about investments at all.

9. Trading in and out. The best form of investment is long term. Take the time to find investments that are going to bring in more money. If you trade in and out of the stock market, there are fees that will take away from the returns, and you might miss out on some gains that those who invest long term enjoy with little to no effort.

What this boils down to is, investing is an important part of your retirement. Without it, you might struggle to survive and find yourself living check to check. No one should count on social security or Medicare to carry them through their retirement years. Invest now so that you have money for your future.

Chapter 3: How to Make Sense of Investing

Investing is intimidating. It is your hard-earned money, and there are all kinds of formulas involved. Investing does not have to be frightening or complicated. When it comes down to it, the subject itself is not difficult to understand. Most people find investing easier to understand when compared with things they are more comfortable and familiar with.

Managing your assets is similar to politics. Whenever there is a major election, the first step is to fundraise enough money to be able to run and get out to see the people. Most of the effort is spent getting that money. It may not seem that way, but it is all behind the scenes. Financial planning is also like building a bridge. It is not necessary to determine the exact weight the bridge can hold. It can be built with room for error, meaning there is no chance it will collapse due to too much weight.

What it boils down to is, investing is scary. For a good majority of us, money was not discussed at home. Investments were not the topic of dinner conversation. Discussing money was always considered taboo, and if that was the case with you, being frightened and unsure is completely understandable. If perhaps you came from a home where finances were not discussed and your loved ones were never financially independent, they might not be the best people to ask about investing. The first investment you make is going to be the most difficult, there is no doubt about it. Once you have gotten past that, investing may never be a breeze, but it will come easier each time.

The goal of investing is to meet whatever financial goals you set for yourself. Whether it is purchasing your first home, saving for an exciting vacation or planning for retirement, the goal is about the hard work. A good goal to have is by the time you retire, you would like to be able to live off of the dividends, interest or investments without having to work a part-time job. If you are going to be working for the next decade or two and want to ensure you will not have to work into your nineties, investing as early as possible is the way to go.

With all the options there are to invest in, that can also be intimidating. The best advice we can give is to do some research and see what is going to be best. There are many factors to take into consideration, your age being one of the most important. Like we have stated before, the younger you are, the more risk you can take. The stock market, money market, and CDs are going to be the easiest (for most people) to begin with.

Whatever extra money you have should be used to pay down debt and invest. We did discuss the importance of having debt paid off before investing and that is key, especially with revolving credit that has higher interest. This can include student loans, especially if the interest rate on those fluctuates, which most do. Over the past several decades, the stock market returns are around 11 percent per year, meaning any interest payments you have on revolving credit above 10 percent needs to be paid off before you invest.

Another important thing to remember is the difference between saving and investing. There are some steps one can take to become a successful investor, which we will discuss a little later. The important thing to keep in mind is that there is a huge difference between savings and investments. If by some crazy twist of unfortunate fate the stock market crashes and you lose your job, you will need a savings account to depend on until you get back on your feet. Do not put all your money into one or the other. Savings is for emergencies. Investments are for the future. You need both.

Investing in general is intimidating. Investing in stocks even more so. A little later on, we will go into greater detail with stocks. For now, know that you do not have to have thousands of dollars to invest in the stock market. There are many ways to get into the market with very little money. Again, we will explore those later. Investing is an important part of your being able to retire at a reasonable age and not worry about how you are going to survive your retirement years.

Chapter 4: Beginning to Invest

There are varying opinions on how to start investing, and here is ours. Investing can be compared to religion. There are people with strong beliefs and actually belong to certain schools of thought when it comes to investing. Here are a couple examples.

1. Gambling Day Traders. These are the people you will see in movies, their desks littered with papers, and their offices holding several flat screen televisions with the stock market on screen. They watch, hold their coffee in hand, and make calls to buy or sell throughout the day, depending on the market.

2. Doomsday Preppers. These are the people who have convinced themselves that the market is going to crash, and therefore put all of their money in precious metals like gold and/or real estate.
3. Indexers. We touched briefly on index investing in the first chapter. Indexers are those who invest in just about everything so that they are able to take full advantage of the steady increases as well as the overall value of the market.

If you already fall into one of those camps, that is totally fine. However, if you have an open mind and would like to learn some easy ways to invest for the long term with no gimmicks, then let us continue and perhaps you will change your mind. In the beginning, it is best to keep the investments as simple as you can. Find a way to be broadly diversified by mixing up ETFs and lower cost mutual funds. You can keep it exciting by holding some individual stocks, but keep it to around 10 percent of your total assets. In order to start investing, there are going to be some choices you need to make.

First and foremost, you are going to need to choose your platform. There are several platforms available to you and below you will find a list.

1. Find an online stock broker. The name says it all, and these people can be found online. In general, you can do almost everything in the way of investing without having to speak to someone on the phone or even meet them face to face. Online

brokers tend to be a little cheaper than the traditional brokers that investors meet face to face.

2. Financial advisors. There is always the option to choose a financial advisor and meet them face to face. Some people do not mind having to pay a premium and meeting the person who will be handling their money.

3. Robo advisors. These are brokers like Wealthfront and Betterment that provide investors with the ease of using online brokers with the benefits of having an actual financial advisor. This type of advisor is gaining popularity and relieves much of the stress when it comes from knowing when and how to invest. What is

great about robo advisors is that the investor is diversified instantly with several different stocks and bonds. Also, the allocations are automatically adjusted regularly based on your financial goals.

4. Investment applications. These are great if you are looking for an easy way to invest with complete automation. With these apps, you do not have to speak to anyone nor do you have to sit down at a computer and research. With an investment app, you can invest for as little as five bucks and get five for signing up. Stash is a great app to check out if you have not already.

5. Direct mutual fund accounts. Using these gets you out of paying broker fees and

you can purchase mutual funds directly from the fund company, in most cases. Owning a mutual fund is a great investment choice on its own, but avoiding fees is also a great way to save money as well.

6. Dividend reinvestment programs. These are also known as DRIPs and are a great way to avoid paying brokerage fees. DRIPs are where the investor directly purchases stock from the company. This is not something all companies do, but several larger corporations do allow it as an investment option. Some companies will also offer incentives if the investor sets up recurring investments or

purchases larger amounts of stocks from them.

With those options laid out for you, we are going to give our advice. Until you are comfortable with investing, look to purchase ETFs or mutual funds either through a direct mutual fund account or an online broker. Always research brokers and find one that not only suits your personal investing needs, but one who comes highly recommended by other investors.

If you have no interest in choosing an individual investment, Betterment has a simple plan aid out for you to get the exposure you need to the stocks and bond market. With Betterment, you choose your risk tolerance, which is shown on a scale of 1 to 10, and it does all the work by investing on your behalf. Money is deposited much like a savings account, making this a simple way to invest.

Finally, if you are looking for that complete ease in investing, check out the Stash app right from your smart phone. Investing with as little as five bucks is a great way to get into investing and begin to feel at ease with the process.

The next step to getting into investing is to choose the account type. You will want to decide whether you are going to invest in an individual retirement account (also known as an IRA) or an account that is taxable. The IRA allows for tax advantages, which is supposed to give the investor incentive to save for retirement. The downside of an IRA is that you are only allowed to contribute so much each year and there are also limitations on when the money can be withdrawn. There are three types of IRAs that we will cover briefly below.

1. Traditional IRA. With this account, contributions might be considered as a tax deduction on your yearly returns. Additionally, the earnings can be tax deferred until the funds need to be withdrawn once you reach retirement age. The main complaint with the traditional IRAs is that the investor might be in a lower tax bracket when they retire. This means that initially, they are probably paying higher taxes with an upfront deduction.
2. Roth IRA. The contributions to this account come after tax, and the money has the potential to grow without tax while

you are saving. The great thing about Roth IRAs is that once you have retired, withdrawing funds has no tax penalties so long as you meet all required conditions that were set up when you opened the account. This is the most highly recommended account to choose.

3. Rollover IRA. This is an account that is opened by rolling over from another account. In general, the rollover comes from a 401k account sponsored by the company you work for. Most people rollover their 401ks into this type of account when they leave their company.

Our advice on IRAs is that if you are new to investing, go with the Roth IRA.

Finally, you are going to choose your investments. This can be the overwhelming part of investing. Initially, you will want to stick with exchange trade funds or mutual funds as opposed to individual bonds and stocks until you feel more comfortable. Mutual funds and exchange trade funds allow you to invest in a wide array of stocks and bonds in a singular transaction as opposed to trading each individual stock yourself.

These are safer investments not only because they are diversified but also because it is actually cheaper to invest in this manner. You will usually pay nothing at all (usually this occurs when you purchase the mutual fund from the company directly), or you will pay one trade commission. Ultimately, if you decide you do want to try purchasing individual stocks, make sure the approach is slow and steady. Do not just jump right in and put all your eggs in one basket. Initially, you will want to invest no more than 10 percent of the whole portfolio in individual stocks until you are comfortable with the process and know what you are doing.

Chapter 5: Stocks and Shares

Before we get into how to trade stocks and shares, let us talk a little about the difference between the two. The distinction can be blurred at times, and the words have been used interchangeably in reference to pieces of paper showing ownership in a corporation, these are known as stock certificates.

Stock is a term that describes those ownership certificates or stock certificates in any given company. Shares refer to the ownership of one particular company. Owning stock refers to ownership in one or more companies. Owning shares means the stockholder has shares in one company. At the end of the day, stocks and shares are pretty much the same thing. The only distinction coming between ownership of stock in several companies as opposed to ownership in one.

With the comparison out of the way, we can talk about how to buy stocks or shares, and you can decide which is going to be best for your financial goals.

First, we will discuss purchasing stocks in four simple steps.

1. Choose a brokerage with low fees and that does excellent research on the market.
2. Think about purchasing stock in companies (remember stocks mean you are investing in more than one) you are

familiar with. This lessens your risk as a first time investor.

3. Consider the number of shares you would like to purchase.
4. Choose the order type. This means select market to purchase immediately or limit meaning you have a price target or maximum.

When choosing your brokerage, there are some things you should consider. First of all, how much money to you have to spend on a brokerage? Most online brokers have a zero minimum requirement in order to set up the account for either retirement or a Roth IRA. Regular brokerage accounts can range anywhere from $0 to more than $2000 to start.

You are also going to want to consider how often you plan on trading. There are commissions that need to be paid to the brokers, and most are about $5 to $10 per trade. Low commission is something to consider if you plan on making more than 10 trades per month. Also, if you are not going to be an active trader, you will want to avoid brokers that charge fees for inactivity.

Next, think about the support level you would like to have with a broker. What do they offer in the way of educational tools, guidance for investing, whether or not there are live people to talk to or if they have branch offices to go to.

Now that you have your broker selected, you will need to decide which stocks to select. This step can be a little time consuming, but when it comes to money, taking your time to find the right companies in which to invest is the way to go. Your objective should be simple. Find companies that you want to be a part owner in. A good place to start your research is the annual report, which is furnished by the company each year. Specifically, look for the annual letter to shareholders. That gives the investor a good ideas as to what is happening with the business.

Next, you are going to take a look at analytical tools and evaluate the business. These tools are available on the brokerage firm's website. There is conference call transcripts, quarterly earnings, SEC filings, recent news, and updates, including financial. The vast majority of brokers will give the investor tutorials as to how to use the tools. Sometimes, you can even find seminars on how to select stocks for your portfolio.

Step 3 in the plan is to figure out how many shares you want to buy. There should be no pressure to purchase any number of shares or to fill the whole portfolio immediately. Start small, actually, you should start really small and purchase just one share. It'll give you the opportunity to get a feel for purchasing shares and give you some time to decide whether or not you want to keep your money with that company. Once you are more confident, start adding to your portfolio.

Finally, choose the order type. Do not allow all the numbers and new words scare you off. Initially, you are only going to want to concern yourself with two types of orders. Market and limit. Market orders say that the investor is going to buy or sell stock at the best and current market price. There are no price parameters meaning the order will be filled completely and immediately. There should be no surprise that the stock market can change from one second to the next. Do not be alarmed if the price you are paying is not exactly what was quoted a few moments prior. Prices fluctuate constantly.

Limit orders allow the investor to have more control over the price that the trade is completed. If a stock is trading at 200 per share and you believe that the shares are worth a little less, the limit order lets the broker hold onto that price and execute the order when the asking price drops to that level. When it comes to selling, the limit order lets the broker know at what price you want the shares to be sold once it gets to that predetermined level.

Now that we have covered how to buy and sell stocks, let's talk a little about how to buy and sell shares. Most commonly, people choose to buy and sell shares through a broker or brokerage service. Investors can also purchase through a prospectus or through a managed fund indirectly.

Purchasing shares is quite similar to purchasing stocks. You are going to find a company (remember share is one company where stock is several) that interests you and purchase shares either directly from the company or through a broker or brokerage firm. You are going to want to research the company and make sure that they are performing well.

Look at their yearly report and see how well they performed over the last couple of years. There is the option to invest in a company that is a startup; however, as a new investor, you are going to want to put your money into companies that are a little more established. That being said, if you are younger and have the wiggle room to take some risks, do so. It is exhilarating to be able to take those kinds of risks.

If you go through a company to purchase your shares and wish to sell it, you will go through the company when you are ready to unload your shares. If you use a broker, let your broker know you are ready to sell your shares, and they will take care of it for you.

Ultimately, there is not much difference between the stock and share when investing.

The purchase and selling of stocks/shares are quite similar. So long as you remember that stock means you are investing in multiple companies and shares mean one, you are going to do just great!

Chapter 6: Futures

Futures are defined as a financial contract that obliges the purchaser to buy or the seller to sell the asset. Assets are usually a commodity or other financial instrument, which were determined for a future price and date. Futures contracts will discuss in detail the quantity and quality of the asset for the futures exchange. Some of these might call for a physical delivery of the predetermined asset, and others are simply settled with cash.

Now that we have defined futures, let's break it down a little further to get a better understanding. Going deeper, futures utilize high leverage in relation to the stock markets. Futures are used to speculate movement of prices for the underlying asset. As an example, corn producers can use futures to lock in their prices and reduce their overall risk. If not, anyone would be able to speculate the movement of price on corn.

There is a slight difference between futures speculation and hedging, which we will cover now.

1. Futures Speculation. Futures contracts manage the potential movement of prices of the assets in question. When investors anticipate the increase of the asset in the future, there is potential to gain by buying the asset in a futures contract then selling it later at a substantial profit. However, the use of a futures contract could also result in a loss for the investor if the price falls

below the original purchase price as specified in the futures contract.

2. Futures Hedging. Hedging is different in that the purpose is not to profit from positive movement. Its purpose is to prevent losses from unfavorable changes in price meaning the predetermined financial result is permitted under the market price. Hedging means someone is producing or using the underlying asset in the futures contract. Gains in the futures contract always come with a loss in the spot market, or this can be the exact opposite. When gains and losses offset each other, hedging is used to lock in the favorable and current market price.

Let's talk a little about the futures contract and how it works so you have a full understanding of it. Futures contracts are legal, binding agreements. In general, they are made on the trading floor of a specified futures exchange. One can also sell or buy particular commodities or other financial instruments at a predetermined price for the specified time in the future. These contracts are standardized which helps to facilitate trading for the futures exchange.

To break it down a little further, some futures contracts are settled in cash while others may require a physical delivery of the asset. In general, futures contract and futures refer to the same thing. For instance, if someone says they bought oil futures, it is identical to having an oil futures contract. More specifically, a futures contract refers to the distinctive aspects of the asset that is up for trade.

As we covered earlier, futures contracts are broken down into two categories. Hedgers and speculators. Those who purchase or produce the underlying asset are hedgers. They guarantee the price the commodity will be sold or purchased at. Portfolio managers are traders, but they can also wager on price movements of the underlying asset through the use of futures.

For the new investor, futures are slightly more complicated and might be something you consider once you get a little more comfortable with investing and trading.

Chapter 7: Options Trading

So far, we have discussed mutual funds, stocks, bonds, and shares in terms of investing. There are so many more options for trading and investing, and this chapter is going to cover options trading. Options are a different type of security, which allows investors to understand the inherent risks and practical uses of this particular asset.

The great thing about options is they are very versatile and they can cooperate with traditional assets like individual stocks. They enable the investor to either adjust or adapt their particular position according to any given market situation that arises. As an example, options are used effectively to hedge against the declining stock market, which limits losses to the investor. Options can be speculated or can be conservative, depending on your level of comfort with risks. Options are a larger part of the overall strategy of investing.

Speaking of risks, options are complex and can be incredibly risky if they are not used properly. Trading options with a broker is advised, and most will provide you with a disclaimer that talks about option trading as being speculative in nature and that there can be considerable loss associated with it.

Options are a subgroup of securities under derivatives. Over time, the word has been associated with huge risks, and it has the potential to crash entire economies. Quite frankly, the perception is overblown. Derivative means the price is dependent on the price of something else. An example of this is wine is a derivative of grapes. Options are derivatives of other financial securities. The value is dependent upon the price of another asset. There are several securities that come under the umbrella of derivatives, which include futures (discussed in the previous chapter), mortgage backed securities, forwards, and swaps. With the 2008 crisis, mortgage backed securities and one type of swap were responsible for the financial collapse. Overall, options themselves were blameless.

It is important to understand how options work if you plan on using them as part of your investment portfolio. If you are unsure of using speculation as part of your strategy, that is okay.

Options can be used without speculation. Whether or not you decide to use options, it is important to understand that the companies you are investing in do use them. Sometimes, it is to hedge risk of transactions (usually foreign exchange), or they will give employees ownership in the company in the form of stocks.

Options cost less than stock, giving them a higher leverage approach to trading that limits the long-term risk of trading. Options can also provide additional income. Options buyers and investors have rights, whereas the sellers have obligations. To break that down a little further, the buyers have the right (without obligation) to buy (also known as call) or sell (also known as put) the stock or futures contract at a certain price, which is good until the third Friday of the month in which it expires. Having discussed calling and putting, it is essential you understand the inner workings of each.

If you choose to purchase an option, there are no margin requirements because the risk is limited to just the price of the option. Option sellers will get a credit into their account for selling the option and will keep the money if the option expires without value. Option sellers will also be obligated to put or call the underlying asset if the option is handled by an appointed option holder. Selling the option is going to require a healthy margin.

In order to trade options, you will want to be well acquainted with terminology from the options market. The price that the underlying stock or asset is purchased or sold if the option is exercised is known as the strike price. Options are made available at different price strikes, which are usually above and below the trading price. Stocks over $25 per share have strike prices occurring at $5 intervals. Those stocks below $25 per share are shown at intervals of $2.

When the option expires, this is known as the expiration date. Stocks usually expire at close of business on the third Friday of the month in which they expire. All of the options have other options that are made available in the current month and the next month. There are also options for specific future months. Every stock has a cycle of months that options are offered in. Each cycle is done quarterly, or at a 4-month interval. The intervals are as follows:

1. January, April, July, and October.
2. March, June, September, and December.
3. February, May, August, and November.

The price of the option is known as the premium. The premium of the option is set by several factors, which include the current market price for the asset, the strike price, how much time is left before the option expires, and how volatile the option is. The option premium price is set on a per share basis. Every option of the stock is equal to 100 shares. For example, if the premium of the option is three, the total premium is 300 shares. Buying the option constitutes a debit equal to the premium into the buyer's account. Selling the option provides a credit of the total amount of the premium into the seller's account.

Options might seem difficult to understand, but they are a great alternative for investors, and there is much more diversity involved. Below is a quick review of how options work.

1. Options allow you to sell or buy the underlying asset or instrument.
2. Should you choose to purchase an option, you are not obligated to sell or buy the actual instrument or asset, it only allows you the right to do so.
3. When an option is sold and it has been exercised, the seller is obligated to deliver the underlying asset or instrument or put the asset at the strike price of the option, no matter the current price of the underlying instrument.

4. Options are only good for a specific amount of time. They will expire, and at that point, you will lose the right to sell or purchase the underlying asset at the previously specified price.
5. Options are purchased at a debit to the purchaser.
6. Options are sold at a credit to the seller.
7. Options are made available at several different strike prices, which are representative of the price of the underlying asset.
8. The cost of the option is known as the option premium. This price is reflective of several different factors which includes the current price of the underlying instrument, the amount of time left until it

expires, volatility, and the strike price of the option.

9. Options are not available with every kind of stock. Currently, there are about 2200 stocks that have tradable options. Every stock option is representative of 100 shares of the company stock.

Chapter 8: Financial Education

In this chapter, we are going to discuss the importance of financial education. In addition, we have discussed risks and, if you are younger, how you should be taking them. However, there is a difference between taking risks and flat out gambling with your investments and ultimately, your profits. Financial literacy is an essential skill needed to build your wealth and enjoy the fruits of your financial labors. The first investment you need to make is in yourself and your financial education.

There are numerous reasons that financial education is imperative to your investing future. Below is a list of seven that we feel are of the utmost importance.

1. Financial education gives you dividends that can never be taken away, nor there ever any loss. With financial education, there is always gains.
2. Financial literacy helps to increase your overall earning potential.
3. Boosts your return on your investments.
4. Secures your retirement.
5. Literacy helps to defend your portfolio from losses that could have been avoided.
6. Gives you peace of mind when it comes to money.
7. Financial education gives your finances and your life more quality.

Most people don't take the time to invest in their financial education because it takes effort and time, and the most common excuse is that they are too busy. If you are going to invest your hard-earned money in the stock market (or any other of the options for investing we discussed thus far), you might as well take a little extra time, put in a little extra effort, and reap the lifetime benefits of financial security and freedom.

Another tip to keep in mind is to be careful who you go to for investment advice. Always do your research before selecting a broker, a firm, or even applications downloaded to your smartphone. There is no reason to jump in head first without fully understanding how investing works. True exports are going to know and understand that when it comes to financial truths, they are complex and subtle. Those trustworthy experts are not going to insult your intelligence by oversimplifying their advice to you.

Keep in mind as well that when it comes to investing, one size does not fit all. There are no secrets with investing. There are numerous ways to invest and make a profit. There are no tricks that are going to earn you money faster, which is where the importance of education comes in. It can be easy to fall for the hype from salesmen wanting to get you into their seminars for which you will pay ridiculous fees. All you need to do is educate yourself and make smart (sometimes slightly risky) investments. You cannot learn which of the several investment strategies are going to work for you from anyone but yourself. No one can tell you that stocks are better than mutual funds because their financial situation will differ greatly from yours.

Everyone brings their own uniqueness to the world and being successful financially is a result of the investment plan that capitalizes on your personal uniqueness. Any advice that is "prepackaged" or "cookie cutter" is not going to help you. There might be bits and pieces that will apply to you. For the most part, it is generalized and you will only learn what works best for you by trial and error. Investment seminars and the like are nothing compared to the financial education you can provide for yourself so that you can find your own, personalized financial truth.

You will also want to be careful of conflicts of interest when it comes to investment advice. The only person who is all in and 100 percent committed to your financial success is you. This is your money. No one is ever going to care more about it than you. Everyone is going to be out to serve their best interest when it comes to finances, and you should do the same. You can avoid conflict of interest by being educated enough to realize the differences between fact and fiction when it comes to investments.

When it comes to your investments, you can delegate authority, but delegating responsibility is not acceptable. Choosing to use a financial advisor or broker is fine. However, make sure that you are not making all of your investments their responsibility. Delegating any issues that might arise to the financial advisor might sound like a good idea. After all, it is the easiest thing to do when something comes up that you have never dealt with before, right? Wrong. Ensuring your financial literacy is going to help you through the difficult investments. The responsibility of your money is on you, not your advisor. The only way you will be successful when it comes to investing is to teach yourself how to do it properly. That includes navigating yourself through the difficult times and learning by trial and error.

Financial intelligence grows like money, and it is important that your intelligence grows as fast as your portfolio. Why, you ask? It is because there is nothing more dangerous than making a million dollar financial decision with a thousand dollars worth of intelligence. Growing your financial intelligence will also grow your wealth.

The return on your investments will improve as you teach yourself to invest smarter, more consistently, and you will eventually learn how to control your losses as well as minimize them. You should make it your goal to deposit regularly into your financial intelligence account, and by this, we mean to expand your mind. Never stop researching.

As we stated a little earlier in this chapter, financial intelligence is not something that can be taken away or lost. Think of it as a one-time investment that continues to pay dividends through retirement. The sooner you invest in your financial education, the sooner you can start earning money. There is so much joy to be found in financial literacy, and it will always be incredibly valuable. Learn to invest and manage your finances on your own, and there is no better time to start than today, right at this moment.

If you need others to help make financial decisions, you are dependent on someone else. Earlier, we mentioned no one will be as committed to or as invested in your financial future as you. There is no reason to become financially dependent on someone else to manage your hard-earned money. There is no true financial freedom if you are dependent on another. Relying on someone else's knowledge is actually detrimental to your financial future. There are thousands of stories about people who amassed a fortune and lost it all because they became lay and ignorant. Financial intelligence is not the same as financial security, and no amount of money is going to change that.

Financial education is by far your greatest investment.

Commit to continuously grow your money. Financial intelligence is not learned in a day, and you need to start somewhere, sometime. The benefits of financial literacy are just as great as the rewards reaped from knowing what you are doing and understanding how investing works.

Chapter 9: Managing Your Money

Let's start this chapter by talking about what money management is. To manage your money means to budget appropriately, save and invest. Even if you have not yet invested anything, you already have the basics of money management. Everyone practices managing their money by making sure they have enough money each month to cover their bills and stash some away into savings. When it comes to managing your money in investments, you can choose to do so yourself or you can use a broker. First timers should check into using brokers or some kind of investing tool to ensure they are making sound decisions when it comes to their investments. This chapter is going to discuss a little of both so that you are able to make a sound decision on whether or not to use a broker.

Between online brokers and all-around easy-access financial information, investing money is as simple as setting up a savings account. The Internet has made it simpler than ever for people to begin investing, so why not take the leap and set up your own portfolio? It's never been easier to manage your own investments. Previously, we talked about finding reputable people to handle your money. This chapter is all about managing it on your own.

It wasn't long ago that purchasing stock meant going to a broker's office and spending hours upon hours going over the stock options before deciding where to invest your money. The order itself went through several different specialists and brokers before the order was finally executed. In 1983, the release of E*Trade changed how we invest our money, and it is incredibly simple.

Online trading has changed how investments are researched, talked about, and transacted. Online trade has made for incredibly liquid markets, which makes it simple to purchase or sell almost any security with the click of a button. Now that we have access to the exact same (and entirely free) financial data brokers do, we are able to set up our own accounts and invest from the comfort of our own home.

As a disclaimer, we should say that just because it is easier does not mean everyone should attempt investing on their own. Perhaps consider using a broker until you feel comfortable. It is easier to lose money than it is to make money, and investing in the wrong stock or business could mean a loss. The tools we have available to us are only as good as the education and experience we have. In the previous chapter, we talked about financial education, and it is still an important part of learning to manage your own money.

The Internet has provided investors with all the tools they need to be able to manage money, but it is important to understand how to use those tools effectively. The following four steps are fundamental to investors wishing to manage their own portfolios.

1. Determine the correct allocation of your assets. Being able to ascertain your personal financial situation and your

ultimate goals for investing is the first thing you need to do in order to set up your own portfolio. There are things to consider like age, how long you have to grow the investments you make, and how much capital to invest in future capital needs. A single person who has just graduated college will have a much different investment strategy than someone who is 50 years old and married. You will also need to consider your risk tolerance and, believe it or not, your personality. How much are you willing to risk for possibly great returns? We all would love nothing more than to reap the benefits of high returns each year. However, if when your investments drop in the short term and you chew your nails to the bed, risky investing is probably not worth the stress to you. Make sure you clarify your situation in the present in order to determine your capital needs in the future. Your risk tolerance is going to tell you how the investments you make should be allocated across all asset classes. Here, you will want to decide if you are aggressive or conservative. Conservative portfolios are set up to protect the value meaning you take less risks. Aggressive portfolios that are moderate tend to take an average risk that will ultimately balance income as well as capital growth.

2. Getting your portfolio going. After you have decided on asset allocation, you will want to divide the capital up within the asset classes. Basically, bonds are bonds and equities are equities. You can break this down further throughout the asset classes and into their subclasses, all of which will have different risks and possible returns. There are lots of ways you can choose assets in order to fulfill the asset allocations. You can choose stocks, bonds, mutual funds, or exchange traded funds (ETFs).
3. Reassess your portfolio weights. After your portfolio has been established, you will want to take a look at it periodically in order to analyze and rebalance where

necessary. Movements in the market can make your original classifications change. Other things that might change over time can be your financial situation, risk tolerances, and your future needs. If any of these things do change, adjust your portfolio accordingly. If risk tolerance drops, reduce equities you hold. If you are prepared to take on greater risks, try placing your assets in the risky small cap stocks. In order to rebalance, you will need to decide which positions are over or underweighted. To clarify, if you have 20 percent of all your assets in small cap equities but your asset allocation says you should only have 15 percent, you will want to make that adjustment.

Rebalancing means you need to decide how much position should actually be reduced and moved to other classes.

4. The rebalancing strategy. When you have chosen what securities need to be reduced and how much, decide what underweighted securities will be purchased from the sale of the overweighed securities. Use the approach we talked about in step 2 to choose your securities. When you sell In order to rebalance the portfolio, always take into consideration the tax implications. If your growth stocks appreciated tremendously and you sold them to rebalance your portfolio, you might be hit with high capital gains taxes. If that is the case, it might be

better to avoid contributing to new funds in that asset class for the future but instead continuing to contribute to other classes. You can also consider the overall outlook of the securities in your portfolio. If you believe the overweighed stocks might fall, consider selling them despite the tax issue. Taking a look at research reports and analyst opinions is a great tool to use in order to gauge outlook on your holdings. Tax-loss selling is a strategy that can be implemented if you want to reduce the tax implications. Always remember that it is important to diversify. While you are building your portfolio, remember to keep diversity. Owning securities in each asset class is not enough. You need to break it down and diversify within all the subclasses. This will ensure holdings within any asset class will be spread out over several different industry sectors and subclasses.

When managing your money, always remember to diversify. It will not be sufficient to own securities in each asset class, you still need to diversify within each of the classes. Make sure that holdings in all asset classes are spread over several different industry sectors and subclasses.

Chapter 10: Ten Easy Steps to Investing

Although many of the things we have discussed thus far may seem complicated, when it comes down to it, investing is pretty easy. All you are doing is putting your money to work for you. This means finding a second job will be entirely unnecessary. The money you are already earning is going to act as that second job or excessive overtime. As we have mentioned, there are tons of ways to invest like bonds, stocks, real estate, and mutual funds. They may sound expensive, but in reality, none of them require absurd amounts of money to be able to begin. So, let's start talking about getting into investing!

1. The first step is to get your finances in order. If you think you can just throw some money into stocks or bonds and it will be fine, you are sorely mistaken. You have to first sit down and take a look at your overall financial situation. Between the cost of living, credit cards, and other revolving debt (car and house payments for example), there is a lot to consider. All of those things are going to take away from how much you are able to invest. Thankfully, investing doesn't take tons of money. You do want to be fully aware of your entire financial situation before you invest. Once you know where your money goes after you get paid, you will be better able to determine how much you can put

toward investments. Remember that investing and saving are two entirely different things. You also want to continue to contribute money to a savings account in addition to investing.

2. The second step is to familiarize yourself with the basics of investing. You do not need to be a financial expert or have an advanced degree in finance to be able to invest. However, you do need to learn the basics. This book has been all about basics, and we have provided you with a good starting point for investing. Make sure you are familiar with basic terms used in investing, so you are able to make sound decisions. Know the difference between stocks, mutual funds, bonds,

EFTs and CDs. Most of these we have already covered in this book, so you should be ready to go. Diversification, portfolio optimization, and market efficiency are things you need to be cognizant of as well.

3. Next, you are going to want to set financial goals for yourself. Now that you have gone over your finances and given yourself an investing budget, you can set a goal for your investments. The goal of all investors is to make money, but that alone should not be your goal. It can be one of your goals, just not the only one. Every investor is different, and their financial goals will vary depending on their personal needs and financial

situations. Some general factors to consider are income, capital appreciation, and the safety of capital. Also, take into consideration your age, personal circumstances, and what position you are at in life.

4. Step 4 is all about risk tolerance. This has been mentioned a time or two, and when we are breaking down how to invest step by step, this is just as important now as it was when mentioned earlier. If the thought of dropping large sums of money into a high-risk company makes it hard for you to sleep, don't do it. You do not want to get stressed out and make yourself sick over an investment. Risk tolerance has a lot to do with age, how much money you

earn, and your financial goals. The older you are, the less risk you should take. Perhaps start out small and take fewer risks, and as you continue to invest, you might find excitement in taking a portion of your portfolio and placing it into something riskier. No matter where your funds are allocated, the market will rise and it will fall. That is the case with risky funds as well. Determine your limits in the beginnIng. If they change over the course of your investing career, that is fine as well.

5. Step 5 covers investment styles. With your risk tolerance determined and your goals set, you need to decide what your investing style is. A lot of first time

investors realize that their risk tolerance and goals are not in line with one another. Conservative investors tend to invest about 75 percent of their money in lower risk or fixed income securities. Those tend to be things like treasury bills. The other 25 percent is usually invested in blue chip equities. Alternatively, aggressive investors put between 80 and 100 percent of their money into equities. With your risk tolerance in place, you should be able to easily decide where to put the majority of your money. As a first time investor, you might consider being more conservative, even if age allows you to take higher risks. Get to know how the market works and feel comfortable with investing before putting money into higher risk stocks and bonds.

6. Understand the costs. In a previous chapter, we talked about financial education. Understanding the costs associated with investing is all part of being knowledgeable. On occasion, some of the costs with investments can cut into your returns. In general, investing passively has lower fees as opposed to active investing. Brokers will charge fees, which will cut into your returns. If you choose to use an investor and are just starting out, check into a discount broker. Their commission charges are less than a standard broker, and you can save some money. Alternatively, if you have chosen

to invest in mutual funds, know that the funds themselves charge management fees. Those are what it costs to operate the fund, and there are some that charge load fees. Like we said, make sure you understand costs and know the different charges associated with investing. That way, there are no surprises when you see your monthly statement.

7. Consider using a broker or investment advisor. Although we talked briefly about some strategies for investing on your own, first time investors should talk to an advisor or broker. It is best to find an advisor that best suits your investment needs. Find a broker who understands how much money you are willing to put

into investing as well as your risk tolerance. Finding the right broker falls under financial education. Don't just go to Google and call the first broker that shows up on the list. Take your time and do some research to find the broker that is just right for you.

8. Select your investments. This is actually the best and most exciting part of investing. If your investment style is conservative, the portfolio will mostly consist of lower risk securities like money market funds and federal bonds. The most important things to remember here are diversification and asset allocation. With proper allocation of assets, the risk is balanced, and the reward is having the

money divided between three separate asset classes. They are fixed income, cash, and equities. When you diversify over several asset classes, you are able to avoid the risk of putting all your eggs in one basket.

9. Remember to keep your emotions in check. Never let greed or fear inflate your losses or limit your returns. There are going to be fluctuations, generally short term, that appear in the overall value of your portfolio. When investing in the long term, you have no reason to panic over those short-term movements. Being greedy can lead to investors hanging on too long as they hope for higher prices, even if the prices fall. As far as fear is

concerned, if the investor gets frightened, they can sell the stock too early. It can also cause the investor to hold onto a stock in the hopes that it will rise even as it continues to fall. We have talked about your investments keeping you up at night. If that is the case, think about your risk tolerance and perhaps consider taking a more conservative approach to your investments, at least until you are more comfortable with the process and taking higher risks.

10. The last step involves adjusting and reviewing periodically. Always review your portfolio and make adjustments as necessary. After you have set up the asset and allocation strategy, you might

discover the weightings have changed. Why would something like that happen? It is usually because the value of your securities within the asset classes has changed. That can be easily remedied with rebalancing.

Chapter 11: Understanding Indexing

Indexing is a term you will hear quite a bit in the investment world. The *index* is defined as a statistical measure noting changes in an investor's portfolio of stocks and is representative of a portion of the market overall.

It is far too taxing to try and track all securities trading all over the country. In order to get around that task, indexing takes a small sample of the market that represents it as a whole. Investors can use indexing to keep track of the performance of the stock market. Changes in index prices tends to represent the exact change in stocks included in that index.

Indexes are meant to weigh companies based on the overall market capitalization. If the market cap of the company is a million and the value of all stocks within a specific index is a hundred million, then simply put, the company is worth one percent of the index. Most of these calculations are done by the minute and are accurately reflecting the trends in the stock market.

Indexes are nothing more than lists of the actual stocks, meaning no one can make one up and use it to steal money from potential investors.

Now that we have discussed indexing, we are going to talk a little bit about the Dow Jones Industrial Average and how indexing works with one of the most well-known and profitable stocks on the market.

The Dow Jones Industrial Average (DIJA) is a mixture of 30 of the largest company in the United States. It is widely recognized and is often referred to as "the market" as a whole.

Dow was created by Charles Dow in May of 1896. Originally, it began with 12 companies and has grown to 30. Originally, it was calculated by average stock prices and today uses the price weighted system. McDonald's is included in the DJIA index and is worth about five percent of the entire DJIA.

The advantages of this index is that it has been around since the late 1800s. Within it are some of the most widely recognized blue chip companies in the United States. It is also not considered risky or volatile, which is great for newer investors. Choosing to invest in DJIA will allow for numerous index funds including the ETF known as Dow Diamonds. These trade under the DJIA symbol on AMEX (American Stock Exchange).

In addition to DJIA, there is the S&P 500, Nasdaq Composite, Wilshire 50000 Total Market, and the Russell 2000 to round out the most popular indexes trending on the market today. Although those are the top indexes, keep in mind that there are indexes all over the world and there are thousands of indexes on every market.

Indexes are great at telling us what turns the market is going to take and which trends are doing well. Ultimately, index funds are mutual funds based on a particular index, and those mutual funds mirror the performance of the mutual fund. Index funds are meant to help beat the market without changing your risk levels. The Efficient Market Hypothesis created in 1975 is where mutual funds came from. Though, it may seem that the point of mutual funds is to get investors to hire professionals who can help them achieve higher returns. Realistically, mutual funds rarely outperform S&P. About 50 to 80 percent of the funds are beaten by the stock market. This tends to happen because of how much mutual funds cost. The return of the fund is the total portfolio return minus any fees the investor pays for the fund expenses and management of the funds.

When it comes to index funds, costs are lower because it is not managed actively. The people who manage the funds only have to ensure the weightings are in line with the performance of the index. This is referred to as *passive management*. Although it is called passive management, the indexes within the portfolio are actually selected actively. For example, when the index changes with the S&P 500, it is almost as if the investor is getting advice from the S&P index committee for free.

It is important to mention that investing in the index fund does not mean that you will never lose money. Over time, the return with S&P 500 has been about 11 percent, which is actually good. With index funds, you are going to want to hang onto them for the long run. Try not to get nervous in a downturn and sell your stock. If so, you might miss the market recovering.

Conclusion

In conclusion, we will leave you with some important things to remember.

1. The very first index was created in the late 1800s by Charles Dow. Over the past 120 years, it has evolved into the DJIA or Dow Jones Industrial Average.
2. The index is able to measure the statistical changes within the portfolio and its stocks that represent the overall market.
3. DJIA uses a measure known as price-based weighting. However, the majority of other indexes will use market capitalization-based weighting instead.

4. The DJIA consists of 30 of the United States' largest companies, and when people refer to *the market*, they are talking about the DJIA.
5. The S&P 500 consists of 500 of the largest companies in the United States. Over time, it has been considered the benchmark of the stock market in the United States.
6. There are other indexes to consider when investing. NASDAQ, which is representative of all companies under the Nasdaq umbrella. NASDAQ consists of mostly tech companies and is one of the most volatile of all market indexes. The Wilshire 5000 has more than 6000 stocks, and of all US

indexes, Wilshire is the largest. Finally, there is the Russell 2000, which looks at the performance of small caps that tend to not be considered in larger indexes.
7. There are several thousand indexes all over the world, and they cover several different regions and world industries.
8. Mutual funds are not intended to beat the market.
9. Index funds expense ratios are lower than most mutual funds. Indexes let investors get into the market and profit from returns.

In conclusion we would like to say that we hope you enjoyed all of the tips provided in this book. Keep in mind that investing is unnerving at times, but putting your money to work for you instead of overworking yourself is worth it.

Thanks again for buying my book. If you have a minute, please leave a positive review.

Thank you!

I take reviews seriously and always look at them. This way, you are helping me provide you better content that you will LOVE in the future. A review doesn't have to be long, just one or two sentences and a number of stars you find appropriate (hopefully 5 of course).

Also, if I think your review is useful, I will mark it as "helpful." This will help you become more known on Amazon as a decent reviewer, and will ensure that more authors will contact you with free e-books in the future. This is how we can help each other.

You can download my other book too. This is the title:

Real Estate Investing: 50 Tips To Get You Started In Successful Real Estate Investing

Here is an excerpt of another book I wrote,

Introduction

You have most likely heard about real estate on and off. By acquiring this book, you are probably thinking of investing in real estate for the first time, or you have the means to invest and would like some necessary information before you begin somewhere.

Firstly, real estate means property which can be in the form of land or a building, and everything else within that said land or building. Real estate investing is the activity centered on making profits from a tangible piece of real estate.

Real estate investing is one of the earliest methods of investments. It has been around since the beginning of human civilization, and back in the days, real estate investing by emperors and monarchies came in the form of conquering lands and colonizing them.

Back to modern times, real estate investing is among the five basic asset classes- shares, bonds, property, commodities and cash and it is a form of investing that is among the most attractive in an investor's portfolio because of its profitability, unique cash flow, and liquidity as well as diversification benefits.

This book will cover everything about guiding new investors in the art of real estate investing. We will be walking over the basics and giving you some in-depth content to the various useful concepts in real estate and also tips and ideas on how to invest in the right property, mistakes to avoid, tax advantages and so on.

But first, the basics.

Chapter 1: The Basics of Real Estate Investing

What is Real Estate Investing?

As mentioned earlier on, real estate investing is the financial activity of operating and investing from a material property, and there are plenty of ways that a person can procure cash flow other than just buying a property and renting it.

The most fundamental form of real estate investing is the investor, otherwise known as the landlord. The landlord purchases a piece of tangible assets, and this can be any property whether a land with a house on it, or just a land, a raw farmland, a land with a building on it or a warehouse on it-- it doesn't matter what the type is. Once the landlord acquires said piece of land, she then finds ways of utilizing the property and usually, it is finding someone who may want to use this property. This someone is known as the tenant.

If both parties agree on renting, leasing or using the property in a certain way, they enter into an agreement. This agreement is called a lease contract or rental agreement. The tenant is then given access to the property or land, and he can use it according to the agreed terms, and according to the agreed length of time. The tenant, in exchange for using your property, pays for the use and this is usually called the rent. Okay- that's the basic, purely fundamental activity of real estate investing. You buy a property and lease or rent it out. You are paid in rental money by the tenant.

For many property owners and investors, real estate investing has a huge psychological advantage compared to investing in bonds and stocks. Real estate investing is a hugely popular form for many investors because investors can drive by their property, touch it, see it, walk inside it, and take pictures of it-- the whole nine yards. The thing is, sometimes real estate investors can become misguided just like stock investors, especially when the stock market bubbles and when this happens, the investor can insist that capitalization rates don't matter.

In a manner of speaking, when an investor can set a price for rental appropriately, then he would be able to enjoy a satisfactory ROI (Return On Investment) on his capital after subtracting the cost of the property, income and property taxes, insurance, maintenance costs and other expenditures. Additionally, always remember that time is your most valuable asset. Calculate the amount of time you need to deal with your investment- this is the reason why passive income is ever so relevant to investors.

Types of Real Estate Investments

One of the key things to do when you start out in real estate is to find your niche. Your niche should be something that you are familiar with. If you are familiar with townhouses, then start there. If you are comfortable with warehouses- begin there. Whatever you do, there are plenty of options in property investments that you can look at that are above and beyond what you are comfortable and familiar with so it could be something to look into once you get the hang of investing.

The major categories of real estate properties are organized according to its unique advantages and disadvantages, its economic distinctiveness and rental sequence, brokerage practices as well as common lease terms. Here are some of the common categories of real estate that you will find in almost any country:

- Residential real estate

- Commercial real estate
- Industrial real estate
- Retail real estate
- Mixed-use real estate

Another way you can get involved in real estate investing is by way of lending:

- You can own a bank that does underwriting of mortgages and commercial real estate loans
- You can provide underwriting private mortgages for individuals, which usually comes at high-interest rates to compensate for the additional risk
- You can also invest in something called mezzanine securities, which allows you to loan money to a real estate development

which you can then exchange into equity possession

Apart from the above, you can also do an extension of real estate investing which is:

- Letting a space so that you have minimum capital tied up in it, enhancing it and then sub-leasing that same exact space to other people for a higher rental rate. This creates incredible returns on capital. An example of space could be a flexible office business venue that allows mobile workers to buy or rent office time
- Obtaining tax-lien certificates. These are a hidden part of real estate investing and not recommended for hands-off or untrained investors. However, with the

right conditions and acting at the precise time, with the right sort of person, it will produce high returns

But above all, the most common real estate investment mostly done by a lot of individuals with significant income would be to own a house and then rent it out.

DISCLAIMER: This information is provided "as is." The author, publishers and/or marketers of this information disclaim any loss or liability, either directly or indirectly as a consequence of applying the information presented herein, or in regard to the use and application of said information. No guarantee is given, either expressed or implied, in regard to the merchantability, accuracy, or acceptability of the information. The pages within this e-book have been copyrighted.

www.ingramcontent.com/pod-product-compliance
Lightning Source LLC
Chambersburg PA
CBHW030813180526
45163CB00003B/1266